Schaum Making Music Piano Library

Rhythm Workbook

Level Four

By Wesley Schaum

Schaum's Pathway to Musicianship

The *Schaum Making Music Piano Library* integrates method, theory, technic and note reading with appealing materials for recital and repertoire. Schaum's well-proven motivational philosophy and sound pedagogy are widely recognized.

FOREWORD

The purpose of this book is to help develop an understanding and feeling for the fundamental rhythms in music. It is intended as a supplement for any level four method book and for students of <u>all ages</u>.

It is intended that all lessons with music notation be <u>played at the keyboard</u>, after the written work has been completed. In this way, the student gets a <u>feeling</u> for the various rhythms plus valuable rhythmic reading experience.

INDEX

Schaum Publications, Inc.

EXCLUSIVELY DISTRIBUTED BY

HAL•LEONARD®
CORPORATION

7777 W. BLUEMOUND RD. P.O. BOX 13819 MILWAUKEE, WI 53213

© Copyright 1999 by Schaum Publications, Inc., Mequon, Wisconsin
International Copyright Secured • All Rights Reserved • Printed in U.S.A.
ISBN-13: 978-1-62906-025-5

Lesson 1. Measures of Different Widths

Name _____ Date _____ Score _____

Music for students is often printed with measures of *equal width*. This makes it easier to visualize the correct note values and number of beats in each measure. However, as music becomes more advanced, measures usually have *different* widths, depending upon the number of notes in each measure.

The two lines of music in this box have the same notes. The upper line has four measures of equal width. The *lower* line has measures of *different widths*. Notice how this saves space, but makes it more difficult to see the note values and rhythms.

DIRECTIONS: The measures below are of different widths. Write the counting numbers on the dotted line below the notes in each measure. Watch for changes of time signature. Be sure to do the Keyboard Assignment (see below).

KEYBOARD ASSIGNMENT: After completing the written work, play all notes at the keyboard three times a day. You may also count aloud as you play.

Lesson 2. 16th Notes in Measures of Different Widths

Name _____ Date _____ Score _____

The sample lines show 16th note counting in measues of different widths.

DIRECTIONS: The measures below are of different widths. Write the counting numbers on the dotted line below the notes in each measure. Watch for different time signatures. Be sure to do the Keyboard Assignment (see below).

KEYBOARD ASSIGNMENT: After completing the written work, play all notes at the keyboard three times a day. You may also count aloud as you play.

Lesson 3. Triplet Notation

The three notes of an 8th note triplet are always connected by the same *beam* (thick horizontal line). Usually, the triplet is marked with a bracket and the italic number *3*. The bracket may be curved (like a slur) or straight. The number *3* may be placed above, below or in the middle of the bracket. Sometimes the *number is omitted*.

The position of the bracket and number varies with the stem direction, the position of the notes in the staff, and the preference of the editor. In the first line, all of the brackets are placed *near the note heads*. In the second line, all of the brackets are placed *near the beams*.

DIRECTIONS: The music below contains triplets. The triplets are marked differently in each line of music. Draw a circle around each triplet group. Also do the Keyboard Assignment (see below).

KEYBOARD ASSIGNMENT: After completing the written work, play all notes at the keyboard three times a day. Watch carefully for the triplets. You may also count aloud while playing.

TEACHER'S NOTE: Counting of the triplet is left to the teacher's preference. As a suggestion, you could use "one-trip-let," "two-trip-let," etc. (the spoken number would depend upon the number of the beat). A three syllable word such as "beau-ti-ful" or "choc-o-late" may help the student to feel the triplet rhythm.

Lesson 4. Finding Triplets with No Brackets

Name _____ Date _____ Score _____

Triplets are more difficult to find if they are marked with a number *without a bracket*. In some music, *none* of the triplets are marked with brackets or numbers.

In music with *many triplets*, the bracket and/or number is often used only for the first few triplets. After that, no bracket or number is used.

In all music, the three notes of an 8th note triplet *always share the same beam*. These samples show various forms of triplet notation with no brackets, with and without numbers:

DIRECTIONS: The music below contains triplets. Many triplets do not have a bracket or a number. Draw a circle around each triplet group. Also do the Keyboard Assignment (see below).

KEYBOARD ASSIGNMENT: After completing the written work, play all notes at the keyboard three times a day. Watch carefully for the triplets. You may also count while playing.

Lesson 5. Accuracy of 8th Note Pairs and 8th Note Triplets

Name _____ Date _____ Score _____

The **main counts** in each measure are the *numbered* counts. For example, in 4/4 time, the main counts are 1, 2, 3, and 4. In 3/4 time, the main counts are 1, 2 and 3.

*The measure below shows how the main counts in a 4/4 measure are divided for 8th note *pairs* and 8th note *triplets*. Notes with *stems up* are triplets. The numbers of the main counts are printed below. Notice that the *first note* of each 8th note pair and the *first note* of each 8th note triplet are *both* on the main counts.

It is important to play the rhythm of the 8th note *pairs* **differently** than the rhythm of the 8th note *triplets*.

DIRECTIONS: The following notes with *stems up* are 8th note pairs and 8th note triplets. The triplets are marked differently in each line of music. The notes with *stems down* are the main counts in each measure. Draw a circle around the 8th notes that coincide with the main counts in each measure. Also do the Ear Training and Keyboard Assignment (see below).

EAR TRAINING: Listen to a metronome set at 56; the tick is for each **main count** in every measure. Next, listen to the metronome set at 112; the tick is for each note of the 8th note **pairs**. Then, listen at 168; the tick is for each note of the 8th note **triplets**.

KEYBOARD ASSIGNMENT: After completing the written work, play the main counts (stems down) with the left hand. At the same time, play the 8th note pairs and triplets with the right hand. If a metronome is available, set it at 56; the tick is for each main count.

*TEACHER'S NOTE: This diagram is intended to show the rhythmic *difference* between 8th note pairs and 8th note triplets. Explanation of two-against-three rhythm should be delayed until a later level.

Lesson 6. Swing 8th Notes

Name _____ Date _____ Score _____

Swing 8th notes are found in some popular music including ragtime, swing, boogie, jazz, rock, show tunes and contemporary pop music. In printed music, swing 8th notes **look the same** as straight (classical style) 8th notes. Although they look the same, swing 8ths are **performed differently** than straight 8ths. Straight 8th notes are all of **equal length**, shown as notes with **stems up** in the treble staff below ("As Written").

In swing style, the **rhythm of each pair of 8th notes is uneven**. The first note of the pair is held **longer** than the 2nd note, producing a swinging or rocking rhythm. To show this uneven rhythm, the 8th notes with **stems down** in the treble staff below are **unevenly spaced** ("As Played").

*The rhythm of swing 8th notes is compared to 8th note **triplet** groups with arrows. The **first two notes of each triplet are tied** to match the longer length of the 1st swing 8th note. The 2nd (shorter) swing 8th note lines up with the last note of each triplet. Numbers for the **main counts** are printed below.

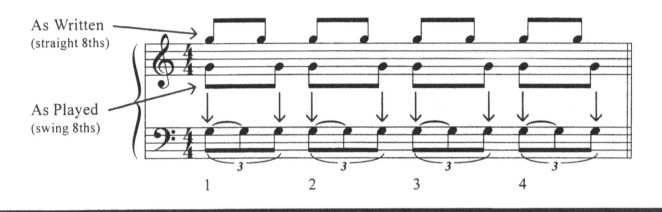

DIRECTIONS: One staff has swing 8th notes spread apart to align them with 8th note triplets in the other staff. Write the numbers of the **main counts** below each measure (see Lesson 5). Draw an arrow connecting the 2nd swing 8th note to the 3rd note of the triplet. Also do the Keyboard Assignment (see below).

KEYBOARD ASSIGNMENT: After completing the written work, play the notes in each line, hands together. Notice that one hand is playing *swing* 8th notes, while the other hand is playing 8th note triplets.

*TEACHERS NOTE: Sometimes, the instruction "swing style" accompanies the tempo mark. There may be notated instruction such as ♫ = 𝅘𝅥𝅮𝅘𝅥𝅮 . When there is no indication at all, the use of swing 8th notes is up to the individual.

Lesson 7. Accuracy of 8th Note Pairs and Dotted 8th+16th

Name _____ Date _____ Score _____

The measure below shows how the *main counts* in a 4/4 measure are divided for 8th note pairs, dotted 8th+16ths and 16th notes. The numbers for the main counts are printed below. Notice that the *first note* of each note group coincides with the main counts. An arrow shows where 8th notes coincide with 16th notes.

It is important to play the rhythm of 8th note pairs **differently** than the rhythm of the dotted 8th+16th note groups.

DIRECTIONS: The notes in the treble staff are 8th note pairs and dotted 8th+16th note groups. The notes in the bass staff are 16th note groups. Write numbers for the *main counts* below each measure. Draw a circle around all notes (treble and bass) that coincide with each main count. Then draw a vertical line connecting each treble note with the bass note *directly below it*. Also do the Ear Training and Keyboard Assignment (see below).

(sample)   1

EAR TRAINING: Listen to a metronome set at 46; the tick is for each **main count** in every measure. Next, listen to the metronome set at 92; the tick is for each note of the 8th note *pairs*. Then, listen at 184; the tick is for each 16th note.

KEYBOARD ASSIGNMENT: After completing the written work, play the notes in each line of music, setting a metronome at 46; the tick is for each main count. You may also play the treble notes alone. Be sure that the rhythm for the 8th note pairs is different from the rhythm of the 8th+16th note groups.

Lesson 8. Finding the Main Counts

Name _____ Date _____ Score _____

DIRECTIONS: The measures below have a variety of note values. Write numbers for the *main counts* on the dotted line below each measure. Draw a circle around all notes (treble and bass) that coincide with each main count. Then draw a vertical line connecting each treble note with the bass note *directly below it*. Also do the Keyboard Assignment (see below).

KEYBOARD ASSIGNMENT: After completing the written work, play the notes in the treble staff. Then play both staffs with hands together. Be sure that the rhythms are accurate. If necessary, refer to Lessons 5 and 7.

Lesson 9. Review of Syncopated Patterns

Name _____ Date _____ Score _____

A common syncopated pattern is shown in each measure below. Each pattern is indicated with a *bracket*. Notice that the *rhythm and counting is the same* in the upper staff and lower staff, although the notation is different. Numbers for the *main counts* are printed between the staffs. These syncopated patterns may occur on other counts and are also found in 2/4 and 3/4 time signatures.

DIRECTIONS: Syncopated note patterns are found among other notes in the measures below. Draw a bracket above each syncopated pattern. Refer to the sample measures above. Write the numbers for the *main counts* on the dotted line below each measure. Also do the Keyboard Assignment (see below).

KEYBOARD ASSIGNMENT: After completing the written work, play the notes in each measure. Do this three times a day. You may also count aloud as you play.

Lesson 10. Syncopated Patterns Crossing Bar Lines

Name _____ Date _____ Score _____

Syncopated patterns may also cross bar lines, as shown below. The patterns are indicated with a bracket. Notice that in every pattern, there is a *tie across the bar line*. Syncopated patterns may cross a bar line in 2/4, 3/4 or 4/4 time.

DIRECTIONS: Draw a bracket above each syncopated pattern in the measures below. Some of the patterns cross a bar line (refer to the sample measures above). Write the numbers of the *main counts* on the dotted line below each measure. Also do the Keyboard Assignment (see below).

KEYBOARD ASSIGNMENT: After completing the written work, play the notes in each measure. Do this three times a day. You may also count aloud as you play.

Lesson 11. 16th Notes and Rests in 3/8 and 6/8 Time

Name _____ Date _____ Score _____

The **8th note gets one count** in 3/8 and 6/8 time. The measures below show how to count in 3/8 and 6/8 time. Notice how the 16th notes are counted. A **16th rest** is indicated with an arrow.

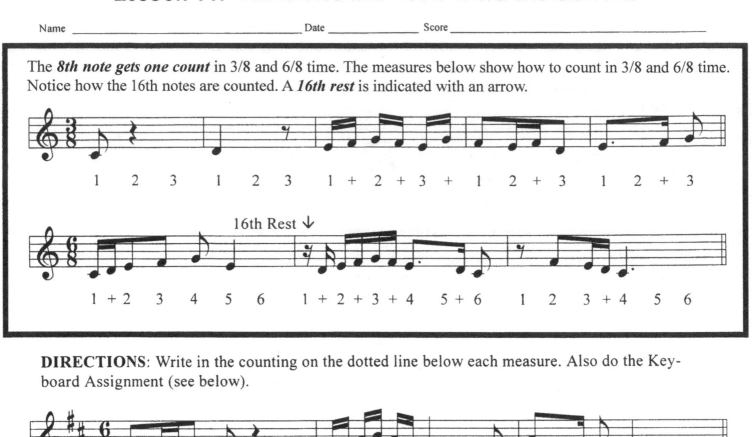

DIRECTIONS: Write in the counting on the dotted line below each measure. Also do the Keyboard Assignment (see below).

KEYBOARD ASSIGNMENT: After completing the written work, play all notes at the keyboard three times a day. You may also count aloud as you play.

Lesson 12. 16th Notes and Rests in 9/8 Time

Name _____ Date _____ Score _____

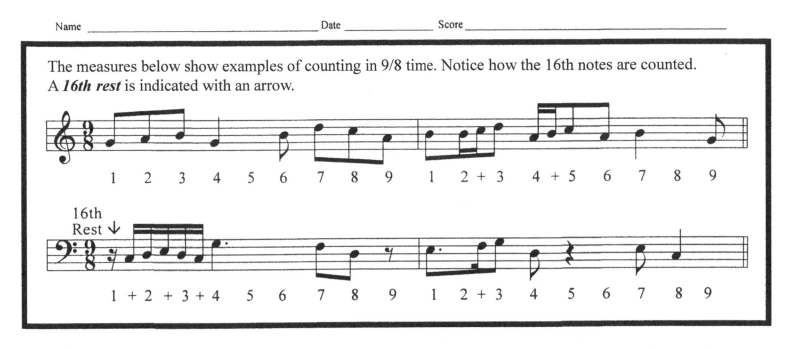

The measures below show examples of counting in 9/8 time. Notice how the 16th notes are counted.
A **16th rest** is indicated with an arrow.

DIRECTIONS: Write in the counting on the dotted line below each measure. Refer to the samples in the box above. Also do the Keyboard Assignment (see below).

KEYBOARD ASSIGNMENT: After completing the written work, play all lines of music at the keyboard. You may also count aloud as you play.

Lesson 13. Counting in 12/8 Time

Name _____ Date _____ Score _____

In 12/8 time there are *12 counts in each measure*. An 8th note gets one count. The note and rest values in 12/8 time are the same as in 6/8 and 9/8 time. The measures below show samples of counting in 12/8 time.

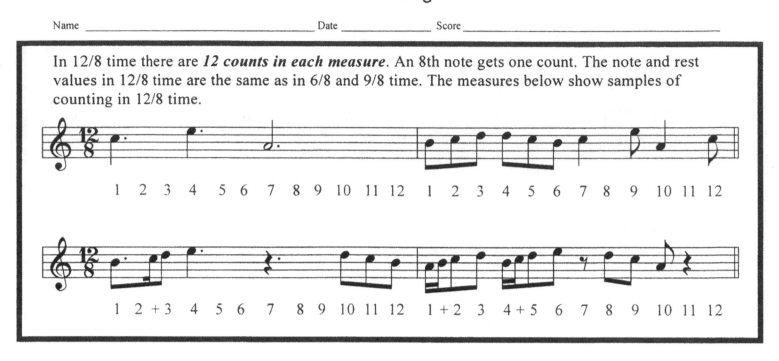

DIRECTIONS: Write in the counting on the dotted line below each measure. Refer to the samples in the box above. Also do the Keyboard Assignment (see below).

KEYBOARD ASSIGNMENT: After completing the written work, play all notes at the keyboard three times a day. Be sure to play the rhythms accurately.

Lesson 14. Counting in 9/8 and 12/8 Time

Name _____ Date _____ Score _____

DIRECTIONS: On the staffs below, some of the bar lines are missing. Write in the counting on the dotted line below each measure. Then draw bar lines where needed so that each measure will have the correct number of counts. Watch for changes of time signature. Be sure to do the Keyboard Assignment (see below).

KEYBOARD ASSIGNMENT: After completing the written work, play all notes at the keyboard three times a day. Be sure to play the rhythms accurately.

Lesson 15. Main Counts in 6/8, 9/8 and 12/8 Time

Name _____ Date _____ Score _____

In 12/8 time the **main counts are 1, 4, 7** and **10**. Some of these same main counts occur in 6/8 and 9/8 time. Except for the first count, the main counts in 6/8, 9/8 and 12/8 time are **different** than in other time signatures (2/4, 3/4 and 4/4). Locating the main counts will help you organize the counting and will make music reading and playing easier. *Vertical lines* indicate the main counts in each sample measure.

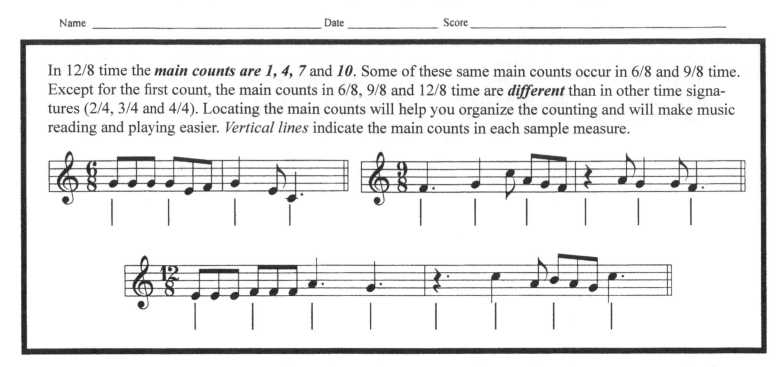

DIRECTIONS: Draw a vertical line under each note or rest where each main count occurs. See the samples above. Watch for changes of time signature. Also do the Keyboard Assignment (see below).

KEYBOARD ASSIGNMENT: After completing the written work, play all notes at the keyboard three times a day. Watch for different time signatures. Be sure to play the rhythms accurately.

Lesson 16. Rhythm Quiz No. 1

Name _____ Date _____ Score _____

DIRECTIONS: Match each musical example with its description by placing the corresponding alphabetical letter on the line beside the description.

A		I	1, 4, 7, 10	_____ Gets 6 Counts in 12/8 Time

_____ Main Counts in 12/8 Time

B		J	$\frac{9}{8}$	_____ Gets 2 Counts in 6/8 Time

_____ Nine Counts Per Measure

C		K		_____ Gets 3 Counts in 9/8 Time

_____ Main Counts in 9/8 Time

D	1, 2, 3	L		_____ 16th Rest

_____ Gets 1 Count in 3/8 Time

E	$\frac{12}{8}$	M		_____ Triplet

_____ Main Counts in 4/4 Time

F		N	1, 2, 3, 4	_____ Syncopated Pattern in 2/4 Time

_____ Main Counts in 3/4 Time

G	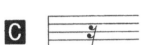	O		_____ 8th Note Gets One Count

_____ Dotted 8th+16th Note

H	1, 4, 7			_____ 8th Rest

Lesson 17. Review of Cut Time

Name _____ Date _____ Score _____

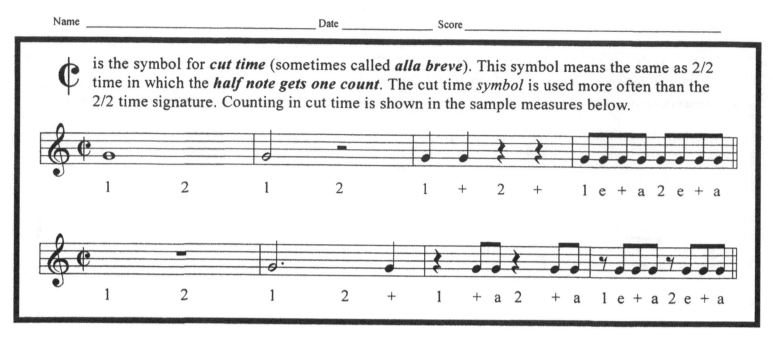

DIRECTIONS: Some of the bar lines are missing in the staffs below. Write in the counting on the dotted line below each measure. Refer to the samples in the box above. Then draw bar lines where needed so that each measure will have two counts. Also do the Keyboard Assignment (see below).

KEYBOARD ASSIGNMENT: After completing the written work, play all notes at the keyboard three times a day. Be sure to play the rhythms accurately.

Lesson 18. Counting in 3/2 Time

Name _____ Date _____ Score _____

Note values in 3/2 time are the same as in cut time. The half note gets one count. The only difference in 3/2 time is the occasional use of a ***dotted whole note***, which gets three counts. Counting in 3/2 time is shown in the sample measures below.

DIRECTIONS: On the staffs below, the bar lines are missing. Write in the counting on the dotted line below the notes and rests. Refer to the samples in the box above. Then draw bar lines where needed so that each measure will have three counts. Be sure to do the Keyboard Assignment (see below).

KEYBOARD ASSIGNMENT: After completing the written work, play all notes at the keyboard three times a day. You may also count aloud as you play.

Lesson 19. Main Counts in Cut Time and 3/2 Time

Name _____ Date _____ Score _____

In *cut time* (2/2) the main counts are **1** and **2**. In *3/2 time*, the main counts are **1, 2** and **3**. Locating the main counts will help you organize the counting and will make music reading and playing easier. *Vertical lines* indicate the main counts in each sample measure.

DIRECTIONS: Draw a vertical line under each note or rest where each *main count* occurs. Study the samples above. Watch for changes of time signature. Also do the Keyboard Assignment (see below).

KEYBOARD ASSIGNMENT: After completing the written work, play all notes at the keyboard three times a day. Be sure to play the rhythms accurately.

Lesson 20. Main Counts in 3/2, 3/4 and 3/8 Time

Name _____ Date _____ Score _____

The **upper** number in all of these time signatures means that there are **3 counts per measure**. The **lower** circled number indicates *what kind of note gets one count*.

3
②
Half Note
Gets One Count

3
④
Quarter Note
Gets One Count

3
⑧
Eighth Note
Gets One Count

DIRECTIONS: Draw a vertical line under each note or rest where each *main count* occurs. Watch for changes of time signature. Also do the Keyboard Assignment (see below).

KEYBOARD ASSIGNMENT: After completing the written work, play all notes at the keyboard three times a day. You may also count aloud as you play.

Lesson 21. Main Counts in Cut Time and 2/4 Time

Name _____ Date _____ Score _____

Cut time means the same as 2/2 time. The **upper** number in 2/2 and 2/4 time signatures means that there are **2 counts per measure**. The **lower** circled number indicates *what kind of note gets one count.*

¢ $\left(\dfrac{2}{2}\right)$ $\dfrac{2}{④}$

Half Note   Quarter Note
Gets One Count   Gets One Count

DIRECTIONS: Draw a vertical line under each note or rest where each *main count* occurs. Watch for changes of time signature. Also do the Keyboard Assignment (see below).

KEYBOARD ASSIGNMENT: After completing the written work, play all notes at the keyboard three times a day. Be sure to play the rhythms accurately.

Lesson 22. Main Counts in Crowded Measures

Name _____ Date _____ Score _____

Measures crowded with many 16th notes or triplets can be played more easily when you find the *main counts*. In 2/4, 3/4 and 4/4 time, the main counts are the ***numbered counts***. The main counts in 6/8, 9/8 and 12/8 time are **1**, **4**, **7** and **10** (see Lesson 15). The main counts are indicated with *vertical lines* in these sample measures.

DIRECTIONS: Draw a vertical line under each note or rest where each *main count* occurs. Some of the measures contain *triplets*. Watch for changes of time signature. Also do the Keyboard Assignment (see below).

KEYBOARD ASSIGNMENT: After completing the written work, play all notes at the keyboard three times a day. You may also count aloud as you play.

Lesson 23. Dotted Half Rest and Dotted Quarter Rest

Name _____ Date _____ Score _____

A dot next to a rest **adds half of its value** to that rest.
A dotted rest is counted like a dotted note of the same value.

A **dotted half rest** is equal to a half rest *plus* a quarter rest.
It is found mainly in 9/8, 12/8 and 3/2 time. It is seldom
found in other time signatures.

A **dotted quarter rest** is equal to a quarter rest *plus* an 8th rest.
It is found mainly in 6/8, 9/8 and 12/8 time, and is sometimes
used in other time signatures such as 2/4, 3/4 and 4/4.

DIRECTIONS: On the staffs below, the bar lines are missing. Write in the counting on the dotted line below the notes and rests. Then draw bar lines where necessary to make the proper number of counts in each measure. Watch for different time signatures. Also do the Keyboard Assignment (see below).

KEYBOARD ASSIGNMENT: After completing the written work, play all notes at the keyboard three times a day. Watch for different time signatures. You may also count aloud as you play.

Lesson 24. Dotted 8th Rest

Name _____ Date _____ Score _____

A **dotted 8th rest** is equal to an 8th rest *plus* a 16th rest. It may be found in any time signature. It is counted like a dotted 8th note. The dotted 8th rest is usually *followed* by a single 16th note, although the order can be reversed.

DIRECTIONS: On the staffs below, the bar lines are missing. Write in the counting on the dotted line below the notes and rests. Then draw bar lines where necessary to make the proper number of counts in each measure. Watch for different time signatures. Also do the Keyboard Assignment (see below).

KEYBOARD ASSIGNMENT: After completing the written work, play all notes at the keyboard three times a day. Watch for different time signatures. You may also count aloud as you play.

Lesson 25. Double Bars and Changes of Time Signature

Name _____ Date _____ Score _____

A change of time signature during a piece is usually
preceded by a **_double bar with two thin lines_**,
as shown here.

These double bars may also be used to indicate a:
1) change of key signature, 2) change of tempo,
3) new section within a piece - such as in a medley,
theme and variations or verse with refrain.

DIRECTIONS: Each line of music contains one or two changes of time signature with a double
bar. Draw a circle around each time signature. Then write in the counting on the dotted line below
each measure. Watch for different time signatures. Also do the Keyboard Assignment (see below).

KEYBOARD ASSIGNMENT: After completing the written work, play all notes at the keyboard
three times a day. Watch for different time signatures. Do not pause at the double bars. The beat
should continue at the same tempo with each new time signature.

Lesson 26. Mid-Measure Double Bars

Name _____ Date _____ Score _____

A double bar may occur in the ***middle of a measure*** for these reasons: 1) to indicate a ***new section of a piece***, such as the parts of a medley, or a theme and variations, 2) to separate the verse and refrain of a vocal solo, 3) to indicate the start of a coda section, 4) to indicate a *change of key signature*. Mid-measure double bars do *not affect* the rhythm or counting.

If there is a ***new tempo mark*** at the double bar, the counting continues at the speed indicated by the new tempo mark.

A measure divided by a double bar is sometimes split between two lines of music. The first part of the measure is at the *end* of one line of music and the other part is at the *beginning* of the next line. When this happens, the beat, counting and rhythm should continue from one line of music to the next *without a pause*.

DIRECTIONS: Draw a circle around the mid-measure double bars in the lines of music below. Write in the counting on the dotted line below each measure. Also do the Keyboard Assignment (see below).

KEYBOARD ASSIGNMENT: After completing the written work, play all notes at the keyboard three times a day. Watch for different time signatures. Do not pause at the double bars.

Lesson 27. Repeated Rhythmic Patterns

Name _____ Date _____ Score _____

Pieces often have groups of notes with the same rhythm. All measures in the sample line below have the *same rhythmic pattern*, indicated with a bracket above the staff. Notice that the intervals and letter names of the notes may be different, though the rhythm and counting are *exactly* the same.

DIRECTIONS: The first measure of each musical excerpt is marked with a bracket. Draw a bracket above other measures with *exactly* the same rhythmic pattern. The intervals and letter names of the notes may be different. *Watch carefully*; the rhythm in some measures is *similar, but not an exact match.*

KEYBOARD ASSIGNMENT: After completing the written work, play all notes at the keyboard three times a day. Watch especially for measures with the same rhythmic pattern.

Lesson 28. Finding Repeated Rhythmic Patterns

Name _____ Date _____ Score _____

DIRECTIONS: Each musical excerpt below has the same rhythmic pattern in several measures. Draw a bracket above all measures that have *exactly* the same *rhythm*. The intervals and letter names of the notes may be different. *Watch carefully*; the rhythm in some measures is *similar, but not an exact match.*

KEYBOARD ASSIGNMENT: After completing the written work, play all notes at the keyboard three times a day. Watch especially for measures with the same rhythmic pattern.

Name _____ Date _____ Score _____

* When a piece begins with an *incomplete* measure, the notes in that measure are called *pickup* or *upbeat* notes. Pickup notes do *not* occur on the first count of the measure. They lead you into the first *full* measure of a piece. Pickup notes can occur with any time signature.

Here are examples of counting pickup notes with different time signatures:

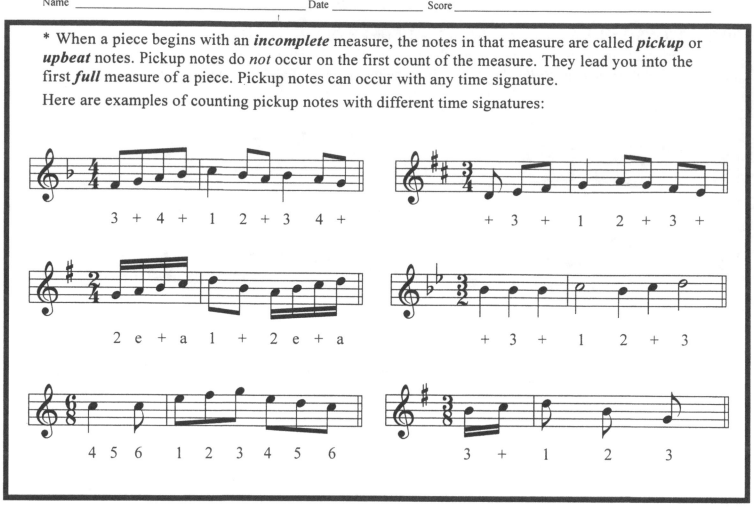

3 + 4 + 1 2 + 3 4 +   + 3 + 1 2 + 3 +

2 e + a 1 + 2 e + a   + 3 + 1 2 + 3

4 5 6 1 2 3 4 5 6   3 + 1 2 3

DIRECTIONS: Each pair of measures below contains pickup notes. Write in the counting on the dotted line below each measure.

*The counts missing at the beginning of a piece are often (but not always) made up in the final measure of the piece. This depends upon the individual composer or arranger.

Lesson 30. Pickup Notes with Missing Bar Lines

Name _____ Date _____ Score _____

DIRECTIONS: Each line of music has pickup notes and one bar line. The remaining bar lines are missing. Write in the counting on the dotted line below the notes and rests. Then draw bar lines where necessary so that each measure will have the correct number of counts. Watch for different time signatures. Also do the Keyboard Assignment (see below).

KEYBOARD ASSIGNMENT: After completing the written work, play all notes at the keyboard three times a day. Watch for upbeat notes and changes of time signature.

Lesson 31. Rhythm Quiz No. 2

Name _____ Date _____ Score _____

DIRECTIONS: Match each musical sign with its description by placing the corresponding alphabetical letter on the line beside the description.

A **I**

B **J**

C **K**

D **L**

E 1, 4 **M**

F **N**

G **O**

H

_____ Dotted 8th Rest

_____ Gets 3 Counts in 3/8 Time

_____ Eighth Note Gets One Count

_____ Half Note Gets One Count

_____ Dotted Quarter Rest

_____ Same As 2/2 Time

_____ Gets One Count in Cut Time

_____ Same Value As ♩.

_____ Gets Two Counts in 3/2 Time

_____ Gets One Count in 9/8 Time

_____ Main Counts in 6/8 Time

_____ Gets One Count in 2/4 Time

_____ Gets 3 Counts in 12/8 Time

_____ Upbeat Notes

_____ Gets 3 Counts in 3/2 Time